Oh, the doors you will open!

HARCOURT SCHOOL PUBLISHERS

STORYtown

Make Your Mark

Senior Authors
Isabel L. Beck • Roger C. Farr • Dorothy S. Strickland

Authors
Alma Flor Ada • Roxanne F. Hudson • Margaret G. McKeown
Robin C. Scarcella • Julie A. Washington

Consultants
F. Isabel Campoy • Tyrone C. Howard • David A. Monti

Harcourt
SCHOOL PUBLISHERS

www.harcourtschool.com

ISBN 10 0-15-343171-7
ISBN 13 978-0-15-343171-5

5 6 7 8 9 10 048 16 15 14 13 12 11 10 09 08

Make Your Mark

Harcourt
SCHOOL PUBLISHERS

www.harcourtschool.com

Theme 5
Where We Live

Contents

Lesson 19

Get Started Story

Social Studies

Science

Theme Writing | Reading-Writing Connection ➤
Student Writing Model: Describing a Thing

6

Lesson 24

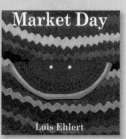

Social Studies

Music

Paired Selections

Theme Big Books

Decodable Books 19–24

READERS' THEATER

Practice Book

"The Princess and the Peas"

Before You Read

Look at the pictures.
Think about what
you already know.

Set a purpose.

I want to find out about frogs.

9

While You Read

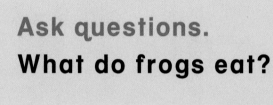

Ask questions.

What do frogs eat?

Reread.

I'll read this page again.

Answer questions.

Oh! Some frogs eat bugs.

After You Read

Retell.

First, tadpoles hatch from eggs.
Then, they begin changing into frogs.
Last, they are full-grown frogs.

Make connections.

This is like another book I read.
I learned how butterflies change.

Theme **5** Where We Live

Artist and title unknown

13

Contents

Lesson 19

1 Get Started **Story**

Beaver's Green Treat

by Nancy Furstinger   illustrated by Alessandra Cimatoribus

2 Genre: Folktale

Little Rabbit's Tale

by Wong Herbert Yee

illustrated by Richard Bernal

Grow, Apples, Grow!

3 Genre: Nonfiction Article

Beaver's Green Treat

by **Nancy Furstinger**

illustrated by
Alessandra Cimatoribus

Beaver dreams of a green feast.
He asks his pals for a green treat.

"Can you offer me a green treat?"
Beaver asks Frog.

"Eat this green beetle," Frog offers.

"Thanks, but I do not eat bugs,"
Beaver squeaks.

"Can you offer me a green treat?" Beaver asks Eagle.

"Eat this green crab," Eagle offers.

"I think it would pinch," Beaver squeals.

19

"Can you offer me a green treat?"
Beaver asks Mouse.

"Eat this green seed," Mouse offers.

"It is too small," Beaver chuckles.

20

"Can you offer me a green treat?"
Beaver asks Peacock.

"Eat this nice, green peach,"
Peacock offers.

"I always eat yellow peaches,"
Beaver brags.

"Can you offer me a green treat?" Beaver asks Seagull.

"Eat this green seaweed," Seagull offers.

"I cannot munch seaweed," Beaver shrugs.

22

"Can you offer me a green treat?" Beaver asks Elk.

"Eat this green treetop," Elk offers.

"That is just the green feast I need!" Beaver grins.

Focus Skill

 Cause and Effect

Learning about **cause and effect** will help you answer these two questions as you read: **What happened? Why did it happen?**

What happened? The bear is getting wet.

Why did it happen? It rained.

The **cause** is the rain. The **effect** is that the bear is wet.

Look at the picture. What happened? Why did it happen?

What is the cause? What is the effect?

 Try This!

Look at the lamp.

- **What happened?**
- **Why did it happen?**
- **What is the cause?**
- **What is the effect?**

GO online   www.harcourtschool.com/storytown

25

Words to Know

High-Frequency Words

dear

sky

mother

told

hurry

door

should

Oh, **dear**! Look at the **sky**! Little Rabbit's **mother told** us it's going to rain. **Hurry**! Let's unlock the **door**. I think we **should** go inside.

Go online www.harcourtschool.com/storytown

27

Little Rabbit's Tale

by Wong Herbert Yee
illustrated by Richard Bernal

Folktale

Genre Study

Folktales are old stories that have been passed down for many years. They usually have a clear beginning, middle, and ending.

> Beginning
> ↓
> Middle
> ↓
> Ending

Comprehension Strategy

Recognize Story Structure

As you read, remember the order in which things happen. What happens at the beginning, in the middle, and at the end?

28

Little Rabbit's Tale

by Wong Herbert Yee
illustrated by Richard Bernal

29

Little Rabbit sleeps under an apple tree. All of a sudden, the wind begins to blow. The branches shift in the wind.

Thump!

Something hits Little Rabbit.

"Oh, no! The sky is falling!" yells Little Rabbit.
"I need to go tell Goose!"
Little Rabbit hops off to find Goose.

31

Goose fishes in the river.
The tip of his rod begins to twitch.
"No time to fish," yells Little Rabbit.
"The sky is falling!"

"Hurry, Little Rabbit! We need to go tell Beaver!"
Goose and Little Rabbit paddle up the river.

Beaver is eating a snack.
Goose peeks in the window.
"No time to eat," says Goose.
"Hurry! The sky is falling!"

34

"Oh my!" says Beaver. "We need to
go tell Turtle."
Beaver, Goose, and Little Rabbit
dash across the field.

Turtle sleeps under a log.

TAP, TAP! Beaver taps on Turtle's shell.

Turtle peeks out.

"No time to sleep," says Beaver.

"Hurry! The sky is falling!"

"Oh, no!" yells Turtle. "What should we do?"
"Let's run back to my house," says Little Rabbit.
"I forgot to tell my mother!"

Turtle, Beaver, Goose, and Little Rabbit run fast.
They hop across the log,
dash across the field, . . .

and jump into Goose's boat.
Then they all paddle down the river.

Little Rabbit hops in the door.
"Mother, the sky is falling!"
"Who told you such a thing?"
asks Mother Rabbit.

"Beaver told me!" says Turtle.

"Goose told me!" says Beaver.

"Little Rabbit told me!" says Goose.

"Well let's just go out and look at the sky," says Mother Rabbit.

All of a sudden, the wind begins to blow.
The branches shift in the wind.

Thump!

Something hits Little Rabbit.

"Oh, no! The sky is falling!" yells Little Rabbit.

"The sky is not falling," chuckles Mother Rabbit.

"An apple just fell from the apple tree!"

"I didn't get to catch a fish," says Goose.
"I didn't get to eat my snack," says Beaver.
"I didn't get to sleep," says Turtle.

"Oh, dear!" says Little Rabbit.

"Can my friends eat dinner with us?" asks Little Rabbit.

"Yes," says Mother Rabbit.

"Hooray!" holler Goose, Beaver, Turtle, and Little Rabbit.

Little Rabbit has a lovely dinner with his friends. After dinner, they all have apple tarts!

Think Critically

1 What caused Little Rabbit to think the sky is falling? CAUSE AND EFFECT

2 Who does Little Rabbit tell that the sky is falling? NOTE DETAILS

3 Why does Little Rabbit want to tell all his friends? DRAW CONCLUSIONS

4 Why do you think Little Rabbit invited his friends to dinner?

MAKE INFERENCES

5 **WRITE** What if the sky was really falling? Write what might happen.

WRITING RESPONSE

47

Meet the Author
Wong Herbert Yee

When Wong Herbert Yee was a boy, he loved to draw. Later, he started writing stories to go with his drawings.

"Little Rabbit's Tale" is his first folktale. "Little Rabbit reminds me of my daughter Ellen," he says. "Her favorite animal is a rabbit. I try to put a rabbit in every story I write!"

Meet the Illustrator
Richard Bernal

Richard Bernal started drawing when he was in the first grade. By the time he was in third grade, he was sure that he wanted to be an artist some day. Richard Bernal says, "I like to have fun when I make pictures. If you go back and look at the artwork, see if you can find the letters R.B. marked on a tree!"

GO online www.harcourtschool.com/storytown

49

Grow, Apples, Grow!

Nonfiction Article

Grow, Apples, Grow!

Every apple tree starts with a tiny apple seed. An apple tree grows roots, which take in water and food from the soil. The apple tree also grows leaves, which make food from sunlight.

apple

seed

In the spring, apple trees blossom, or grow flowers.

The flowers drop off, and apples grow in their place.

In the fall, the apples are ready to be picked.

People make many kinds of foods from apples.

Apples may be sweet, or tart,
or soft, or crisp, or crunchy.
But one thing apples always are is

munchy, munchy, munchy!

Connections

Comparing Texts

1 How are the story and the article the same?

2 What things can really fall from the sky?

3 Would you act like Little Rabbit if something hit your head? Why or why not?

Writing

Little Rabbit was very silly to think the sky was falling. Write about something silly you have done.

One day I wore two different shoes to school. I was in a hurry. Everyone laughed at my shoes. It was funny.

Phonics

Make and read new words.

Start with **me**.

Add [a] [n] to the end.

Change [m] to [b].

Take away [a] [n].

Add [e] [p] to the end.

Fluency Practice

Read the story aloud with a partner. Try to read the words smoothly. You will see the sentence <u>The sky is falling!</u> a lot. When you read this sentence, point up to the sky.

Reading-Writing Connection

Describing a Thing

In "Little Rabbit's Tale," an apple falls and hits Little Rabbit. After I read the story, I wrote a description of an apple. Here is what I wrote.

Student Writing Model

My Favorite Apples
by Charles

My favorite apples are the green ones. Their skin is smooth and shiny. They are crispy and crunchy. They taste sweet and sour at the same time. That is why I like them.

Writing Trait
VOICE I tell how I feel about my topic.

Writing Trait
WORD CHOICE I use words that tell how the apple looks, feels, sounds, and tastes.

This is what I do when I write.

▶ **I write my ideas.**

apple

rabbit

turtle

sky

▶ **I choose the idea that I like best.**

▶ **I plan my writing.**

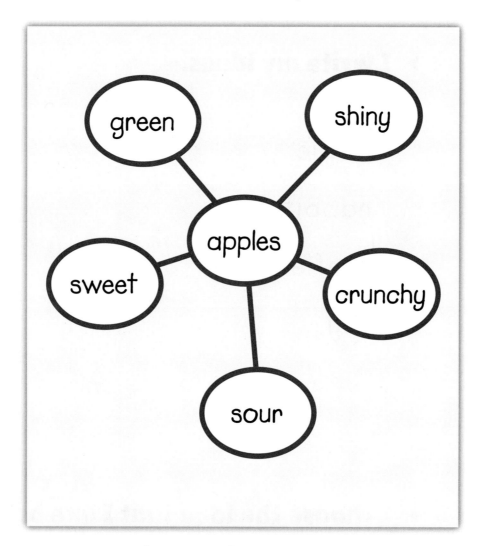

▶ **I write my ideas.**

▶ **I read my writing and make changes.**

56

Here are some things to remember when you write a description.

Checklist for a Description

☐ I write about just one topic.

☐ I describe my topic so readers can picture it in their mind.

☐ My sentences begin with capital letters.

☐ My sentences end with the right end marks.

☐ I use complete sentences.

Contents

Lesson 20

1 Get Started Story

Kids Play!
by Sandra Widener

2 Genre: Nonfiction

Ways People Live
by Emily Neye

Houses

by Aileen Fisher
Illustrated by David Gordon

3 Genre: Poetry

59

Phonics
Words with <u>ai</u>
and <u>ay</u>

Words to Know

Review

over

sky

hurry

other

would

Kids Play!

by Sandra Widener

Kids from all over play. From Spain to
New York, kids spend days playing.

Stay in a park and see kids on swings.
Kids pump their legs back and forth
and swing way up into the sky.

Whee!

Kids can run and leap and do flips all day! Kids play leapfrog and have fun in their backyards.

One, two, three, **leap!**

Kids like to play hopscotch. In this park,
kids play hopscotch like this. They hop one
hop at a time.

Hop! Hop!

Kids think of lots of ways to play. See all of them jump and play! They think jumping is fun!

Swish! Swish!

Kids play with balls. Show up with a ball,
and kids will hurry to play. Just wait! Kids
will kick that ball back into the sky.

See that ball sail!

Kids ask, "May I play?"

Other kids say, "Yes! Let's play!"

Would you like to play, too?

Focus Skill

 Cause and Effect

Learning about **cause and effect** will help you answer these two questions as you read: **What happened? Why did it happen?**

What happened? The ice cream is melting.

Why did it happen? Because it's hot out.

The **cause** is the heat. The **effect** is that the ice cream is melting.

Look at the picture.

- **What happened?**
- **Why did it happen?**

- **What is the cause?**
- **What is the effect?**

 Try This!

Look at the car.

- **What happened?**
- **Why did it happen?**

- **What is the cause?**
- **What is the effect?**

GO online www.harcourtschool.com/storytown

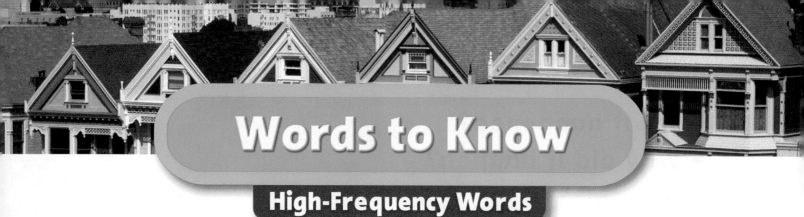

Words to Know

cool

warm

dry

place

holes

four

move

where it is wet
and where it is dry.

Dry Places

In the desert, the air is very dry. Rain will not fall for many weeks. The air is hot in the daytime but cold at night.

People dress like this.
Their clothes keep the
sun and sand off their skin.

Look at the homes. The bricks are made of sand and mud.

Clip-Clop, Clip-Clop!

Sometimes camels bring people across the desert. They carry food and tents on their backs.

Wet Places

In the rain forest, the air is hot. The rain forest is not dry like the desert. Sometimes it rains for weeks!

80

People dress like this. Their clothes help them stay cool.

People pick nuts from the trees. They catch fish to eat, too.

When a lot of rain falls, there's water everywhere! That's why many houses are up on stilts.

Splish, Splash!

Children like to play by the water. Some children like to play by the waterfall. It's fun to play on the rocks, too!

83

Cold Places

In the Arctic, the air is very cold! This is a land of ice and snow. It is cold much of the time.

People dress in warm clothes.

People live in houses that keep out the cold wind.

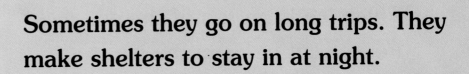

Sometimes they go on long trips. They make shelters to stay in at night.

Thick ice is on top of the water. People cut holes in the ice to catch the fish down below. Some people sell the fish at the market.

It is hard to move on deep snow.
Some people use snowshoes.

This man has a faster
way! Does this look like
fun to you?

Crunch, Crunch!

Places with Four Seasons

Winter

Spring

Here there are four seasons —
winter, spring, summer, and fall.

Summer

Fall

In the winter, the air is cold.
People dress in hats and coats.
Snow falls, but it will melt soon.

In spring and summer, the air gets warmer. People dress in shirts and shorts. Many like to sail and swim.

Houses like this keep out the heat in the summer. They keep out the cold in the winter, too. Houses like this are needed in places with four seasons.

Crickle, Crackle!

Now the season is fall. Children have fun playing in the leaves.

People like to have fun no matter where they live. What do you do for fun in the **place** where you live?

Think Critically

1 Why do people dress in different ways in different places? CAUSE AND EFFECT

2 Why are there so many different kinds of houses? MAKE INFERENCES

3 What might people do for fun in the Arctic? DRAW CONCLUSIONS

4 How do camels help some people in the desert? NOTE DETAILS

5 **WRITE** What is your favorite kind of weather? Write about why you like it. WRITING RESPONSE

About the Author
Emily Neye

Emily Neye has written many books for children. She likes writing nonfiction best. "I like to write about real things," she says. "There is so much to learn about the world."

"I liked writing this story. It was fun to think about what it would be like to live in faraway places. I visited the rain forest once and saw huge plants. They were amazing!"

GO online www.harcourtschool.com/storytown

Houses

by Aileen Fisher
Illustrated by David Gordon

Poetry

Houses

by Aileen Fisher
illustrated by David Gordon

Houses are faces
(haven't you found?)
with their hats in the air,
and their necks in the ground.
Windows are noses,
windows are eyes,
and doors are the mouths
of a suitable size.
And a porch—or the place where
porches begin—
is just like a mustache
shading the chin.

95

Connections

Comparing Texts

① How are the story and the poem the same? How are they different?

② What kinds of weather have you seen?

③ What house in the story would you like to visit? Tell why.

Ways People Live
by Emily Neye

Houses
by Aileen Fisher
Illustrated by David Gordon

Writing

There are many kinds of houses in the story. Write about a house you would like to live in. Tell about the color, size, and shape of the house.

My house would have a round room in the middle. It would also have

Make and read new words.

Start with **chain**.

Change **c** **h** to **m**.

Change **i** **n** to **y**.

Change **m** to **d**.

Add **s** to the end.

Fluency Practice

Read with a partner. Take turns reading each page of the story. Many sentences begin with:

In the _____.

Read these sentences together along with your partner.

Contents

Lesson 21

1 Get Started Story

The Missing Cake

by Sandra Widener • illustrated by Valeria Cis

2 Genre: Play

Flake, the Missing Hamster

by Stephen Krensky
illustrated by Susanna Natti

3

Three Reasons Why Pets Are Great

Genre: Nonfiction Article

Phonics
Words with a-e

Words to Know

Review

warm

cool

over

our

mother

told

The Missing Cake

by Sandra Widener

illustrated by
Valeria Cis

Dale made a cake with Mom. He set the warm cake on a plate to cool. Then he added whipped cream to the top. It was simple and fun!

Jane came over to eat the cake with Dale. He wanted to show Jane how he made the cake. "Oh, no!" Dale yelled. "Our cake is not on the plate!"

Dale and Jane looked at that clean plate. "Where is our cake? asked Dale. "This is a big mess!"

Dale asked his mother about the cake.
She told him she didn't know.

"Oh!" she groaned. "That was your treat."

Dale asked Dad the same thing.
"That cake is missing?" asked Dad. "What
a shame! I didn't get to taste that cake."

Then, Dale and Jane looked for Jade.
Jade was napping by the window.
She looked up and wagged her tail.

106

Jade had bits of cake on her.
"You smell like cake!" Dale grinned. "Well, at least that cake tasted good to you!"

Phonics Skill

Words with a-e

The letter **a,** followed by a consonant and **e,** can stand for the long <u>a</u> sound as in **skate, plane,** and **lake**.

skate

plane

lake

108

**Look at each picture. Read the words.
Tell which word names the picture.**

can

cane

cone

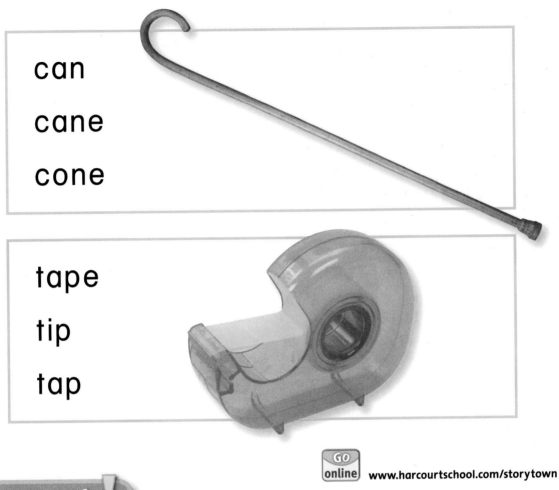

tape

tip

tap

GO online www.harcourtschool.com/storytown

Try This!

Read the sentences.

Jake and Dave play a game of tag. They run to the gate. The gate is the base. Run Jake and Dave!

Words to Know

found

near

hears

might

open

gone

around

tired

I am a hamster. I **found** a nice place to live. I like to be **near** children. "Squeak, squeak!" I think the class **hears** me! The children **might open** my door and pet me. Soon they will be **gone**. Then I will run **around** on my wheel. At night I'll get **tired** and go to sleep.

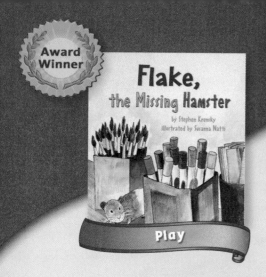

Flake,
the Missing Hamster
by Stephen Krensky
Illustrated by Susanna Natti

Play

Genre Study

A **play** is a story that is written to be acted out. What the characters say to each other tells the story.

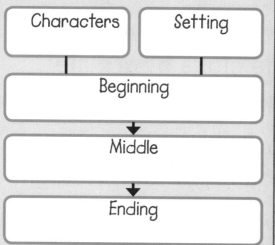

Characters	Setting

Beginning

↓

Middle

↓

Ending

Comprehension Strategy

Summarize As you read, stop and think about what has already happened.

Flake,

the Missing Hamster

by Stephen Krensky
illustrated by Susanna Natti

Narrator: One day Lionel went to feed Flake. Flake was the class hamster. He lived near the window.

Lionel: Oh, no!

Miss Sanchez: What's wrong, Lionel?

Lionel: The door is open. Flake is gone!

Jeffrey: Oh, no! Flake, Flake! Where are you, Flake?

Gwen: Where can he be?

Kate: What can we do?

Miss Sanchez: We just need to find Flake fast. Let's all start looking.

Narrator: The class looked everywhere for the hamster. They looked under the desks. They looked on the bookshelf. They even looked in the trash can.

Jeffrey: Lionel, why are you looking in the trash can? What would Flake be doing in there?

Lionel: Maybe he fell in by mistake.

Narrator: The class found three pens and a ball. They didn't find Flake.

Lionel: What if we all squeak like hamsters? When Flake hears us, he will squeak, too. Then we can find him.

Gwen: Squeak!

Jeffrey: Hamsters don't squeak like that! Hamsters squeak like this. Squeak, squeak!

Kate: Squeak, squeak, squeak!

Gwen: This isn't working.

121

Jeffrey: Roar!

Lionel: Roar? Why did you roar? Hamsters don't roar!

Jeffrey: I know. But what if Flake is sleeping? A roar would wake him up.

Kate: I don't know how brave Flake is. He might think a big animal is out here waiting to get him.

Jeffrey: I didn't think of that.

Gwen: What if we start to play like hamsters? Flake will see us. Then he will come out and play, too.

Narrator: So everyone ran around like hamsters. Kate and Gwen sniffed the air. Then Lionel started running in place.

Kate: What are you doing?

Lionel: I'm running the way Flake runs on his wheel. It's a lot of work. I'm getting tired!

Narrator: They played some more, but Flake did not come out.

Jeffrey: This is not working.

Gwen: What should we do now?

Miss Sanchez: Let's stop looking for Flake now. Maybe we'll think better after we have our snacks.

Narrator: So the class got out their snacks and started to eat.

Lionel: All that running made me very hungry. If I were Flake, I would get hungry a lot.

127

Narrator: Just then a little head popped out by some books. Then the head came out a little more.

Jeffrey: Look, everyone! It's Flake! I'll get him.

Kate: I bet he wants a snack, too.

Lionel: Oh, Flake! You're safe now!

Miss Sanchez: I always like a happy ending.

129

Gwen: Hooray for Flake, the hungry hamster!

All: Hooray for Flake!

Think Critically

1. What is the problem? How is it solved? PROBLEM/SOLUTION

2. Which ideas for finding Flake were silly? MAKE INFERENCES

3. How can you tell that the children are good listeners? DRAW CONCLUSIONS

4. Why do you think Flake came out? MAKE INFERENCES

5. **WRITE** How did the class try to find Flake? Tell how you know from the story. WRITING RESPONSE

Meet the Author
Stephen Krensky

Lionel is a character in many of Stephen Krensky's books. This is the first play about Lionel that Mr. Krensky has written.

"I enjoyed writing the play," says the author. "It was a way to get Lionel off the printed page. Children can make him real! We never had a hamster when I was in school."

Meet the Illustrator
Susanna Natti

Susanna Natti illustrates all of Stephen Krensky's Lionel stories. She also illustrates many other books.

"It was fun to illustrate this play! I laughed out loud when I read about Lionel and his friends squeaking and running around like hamsters."

chickaDEE

Discover a World of Fun · October 2003

Join the **PET PARTY**

Balls of Fun

Make your pet a ___

Nonfiction Article

Three Reasons Why Pets Are Great

1 Pets Make Great Friends

All kinds of animals make fun friends! Most dogs are friendly and love to play with their owner. All you need to do is feed them, brush them and best of all, play with them. Then your pet will be your best pal!

2 Pets Teach You to Take Care of Something

No matter how big or small your pet is, taking care of it is a big job. Even small and fuzzy hamsters take work. They always need fresh food and water and their cage has to be cleaned every week.

3 Pets Are Fun

Best of all, pets are fun. Some pets always do silly things, like lick your face or tickle you. Pets can make everyone happy!

135

Connections

Comparing Texts

❶ How are the story and the article the same? How are they different?

❷ What other animals make good pets?

❸ What kind of class pet would you like to have? Tell why.

Writing

In the story, a hamster gets lost. Write about another animal that gets lost. Your story can be real or make-believe.

One day, we couldn't find our cat, Bubbles. We looked and looked. Then we found her in the closet with her new kittens.

136

Make and read new words.

Start with **tape**.

Change **t** to **s** **h**.

Change **s** **h** to **c**.

Change **p** to **n**.

Change **n** to **k**.

Fluency Practice

Read with a group. Each person can read a different part. Use your voice to show how the character feels. The characters should sound worried at the beginning. They should sound happy at the end.

Contents

Lesson 22

1 Get Started **Story**

Mike and Spike Hike
by Sandra Widener
illustrated by Andre Letria

2 Genre: Fantasy

We're Going on a Picnic!

PAT HUTCHINS

Beaks Eat
art by Diane Blasius

3 Genre: Nonfiction Article

Phonics
Words with i-e

Words to Know

Review

warm

near

cool

should

Mike and Spike Hike

by Sandra Widener

illustrated by Andre Letria

140

"It is a lovely, fine day," said Mike.

"Yes, and the sunshine is warm," said Spike.
"Let's go on a hike. We can hike all day."

141

Mike and Spike arrive at the site.

"You cannot fly a kite on a hike!" said Mike.

"You cannot ride a bike on a hike!" said Spike.

Mike will ride his bike for miles and miles.
Spike will fly his kite until bedtime. Then
Mike and Spike will hike at sunrise.

143

The next day, Mike and Spike arrive at the site.
"You cannot drive near me on a hike!" said Mike.

"You cannot dive and glide on a hike!" said Spike.

Mike will dive and glide until bedtime.

Spike will drive for miles and miles.

Then Mike and Spike will hike at sunrise.

145

The next day, Mike and Spike arrive at the site. "Look!" said Mike, "It could rain, and it is too cool."

"Maybe we should not hike here," said Spike.

Mike and Spike will not hike today. They will hike at sunrise on a lovely, warm day.

Phonics Skill

Words with i-e

The letter **i** can stand for the long <u>i</u> sound in the middle of the words **vine**, **dime**, and **lime**.

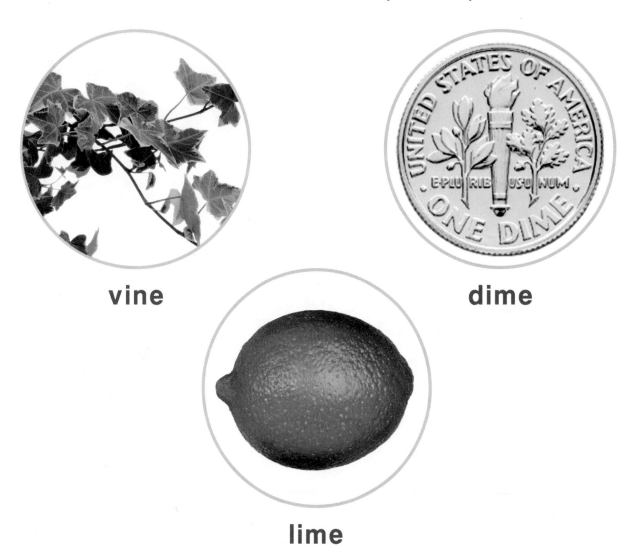

vine

dime

lime

Look at each picture. Read the words.
Tell which word names the picture.

back

bake

bike

kit

kite

coat

 www.harcourtschool.com/storytown

Try This!

Read the sentences.

I like to ride my bike. I ride
all the time. I can ride five
miles on my bike. Do you like
to ride your bike?

walked

light

because

those

right

Hen had a new basket. She **walked** over to show her friends.

"That's a nice basket," said Duck. "It's so **light**."

"That's **because** there's no food in it," said Hen. "Let's fill it with **those** apples."

"All **right**," said Duck. "We will fill it to the top!"

We're Going on a Picnic!

PAT HUTCHINS

Fantasy

Genre Study

A **fantasy** is a make-believe story about something that could never happen. In fantasies, animal characters sometimes have problems that they try to solve in silly ways.

Problem	Solution

Comprehension Strategy

Ask Questions As you read, ask yourself questions to be sure you understand the story.

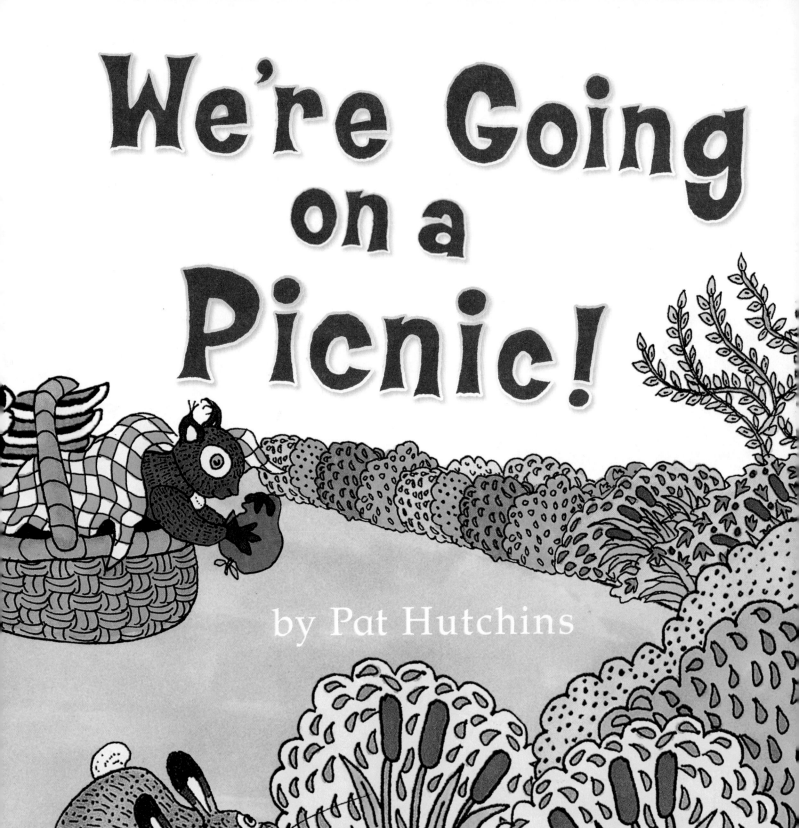

We're Going on a Picnic!

by Pat Hutchins

"Let's go on a picnic," said Hen, Duck,
and Goose. "It's such a lovely day!"
So Hen picked some berries
(because Hen liked berries best),
and Goose picked some apples
(because Goose liked apples best),
and Duck picked some pears
(because Duck liked pears best).
And they put them in the basket.

155

"We're going on a picnic!" they sang
as they walked across the field.

"This looks like a nice place
for a picnic," said Hen,
and set the basket down.
"I can't wait to eat
some of those berries!"

158

"It's a bit shady," said Duck.
"Let's go up the hill.
We might find an even nicer place."
"All right," said Hen,
"but it's your turn to carry the basket."

"We're going on a picnic!" they sang
as they walked up the hill.

"This looks like a nice place for a picnic,"
said Duck, and set the basket down.
"I can't wait to eat some of those pears!"

"It's a bit windy," said Goose.
"Let's go down the hill.
We might find an even nicer place."
"All right," said Duck,
"but it's your turn to carry the basket."

"We're going on a picnic!" they sang
as they walked down the hill.

"This looks like a nice place for a picnic,"
said Goose, and set the basket down.
"I can't wait to eat some of those apples!"
"It's a bit hot," said Hen and Duck.
"Let's go down this path.
We might find an even nicer place."
"All right," said Goose,
"but let's ALL carry the basket."

"We're going on a picnic!" they sang
as they walked around the lane.

"Oh!" they cried,
and set the basket down.
"We've walked back home,
and we haven't had our picnic!"

"Off we go again," said Hen.
But when they picked up the basket,
it was very light.

And very empty.

"Duck," said Hen, "did you eat the pears?"

"No," said Duck.

"Goose," said Hen, "did you eat the apples?"

"No," said Goose.

"Hen," said Duck and Goose, "did you eat the berries?"

"No," said Hen.

"Then they must have fallen out," said everyone at the same time.

So Hen picked some more berries
(because Hen liked berries best),
and Goose picked some more apples
(because Goose liked apples best),
and Duck picked some more pears
(because Duck liked pears best).
And they put them in the basket.

"We're going on a picnic!" they sang
as they walked across the field.

173

"This looks like a nice place for a picnic," they all said, and set the basket down.

Think Critically

1 What is the problem in the story?

PROBLEM/SOLUTION

2 What happened to the food? DETAILS

3 What is the same about Hen, Duck, and Goose? MAKE INFERENCES

4 Did the animals find out who took their food? How do you know?

DRAW CONCLUSIONS

5 **WRITE** Write about a perfect picnic spot. Use describing words. WRITING RESPONSE

175

Meet the Author and Illustrator
Pat Hutchins

Pat Hutchins grew up in the country. "All around us were fields and woods full of wildlife," she says. "We spent many hours watching the animals and birds." Pat Hutchins started drawing when she was very young. Two of her favorite things to do are to paint and to watch birds.

GO online www.harcourtschool.com/storytown

Feathered friends

Nonfiction Article

Beaks Eat

art by Diane Blasius

toucan

Birds don't have fingers and they don't have teeth. How do they pick things up? How do they eat?

They use their beaks.

Beaks are tough and strong. They can dig holes and crack nuts and cut meat.

Beaks are sensitive, like human fingertips. They can feel when they touch a worm underground, or even when a worm wiggles in the dirt nearby.

crossbill

goldfinch

sparrow

Beaks come in all shapes and sizes, but every bird has a beak. They use their beaks to crack open the shell of the egg when they're hatching. They use their beaks to build their nests, to clean their feathers, and to carry food to their babies.

But mostly, birds use their beaks to eat.

Connections

Comparing Texts

1 How are Hen, Goose, and Duck like the birds in "Beaks Eat"?

2 What are some good places to have a picnic?

3 What would you like to eat on a picnic?

Writing

The characters in the story bring their favorite foods on their picnic. Make a list of your favorite foods. Tell why you like them.

Phonics

Make and read new words.

Start with **time**.

Change [t] to [d].

Change [d] to [l].

Change [m] to [k].

Change [l] to [b].

Fluency Practice

Make up a voice that sounds like a duck. Use that voice when you read Duck's part. Make up voices for Hen and Goose, too.

181

Contents

Lesson 23

1 **Get Started Story**

Hang on, Rose!
by Sandra Widener
Illustrated by Steve Adams

2 **Genre: Nonfiction**

On Saturday
by Nina Crews

3 **Genre: Nonfiction Article**

The River city

Phonics
Words with o-e

Words to Know

Review

warm

opened

around

found

walked

Hang on, Rose!

by Sandra Widener
illustrated by Steve Adams

184

Rose and Chad sat on the steps. The day
was warm, but Rose was not happy. She
laid her nose on Chad's lap.

Chad spoke to Rose. "Would you like to play?"

Rose just sat there.

Chad opened his bag and poked around. "I found this big, red apple just for you!" Chad smiled.

Rose sniffed the apple, but she was not happy.

Then Dan walked by. "That apple looks good," he said. "I will trade a jump rope for it."

Rose looked away.

Then Jane stopped by.
"Is that a jump rope?" she asked. "I
will trade this ice cream cone for it."

Rose sneezed.

189

Sam rode up and said, "An
ice cream cone! Can I eat it?"

"Yes," Chad said, "but we
need something for Rose."

"I know!" Sam grinned.
"Hang on, Rose!"

Sam came back with a big bone that made Rose sit up. She jumped and her tail wagged back and forth. She chomped on that bone and then thanked Chad with a big, wet kiss!

Focus Skill

 Draw Conclusions

Sometimes readers must use clues to figure things out in stories. Figuring things out this way is called **drawing conclusions.**

In this picture we can draw the conclusion that the children are walking to school.

Clues:

• They have books.

• There are school buses in front of the building.

Look at the picture.

What is your conclusion? What clues helped you?

Look at the picture.
What is your
conclusion?
What clues
helped you?

 www.harcourtschool.com/storytown

193

Words to Know

High-Frequency Words

- love
- city
- hello
- loudly
- brown
- pulled

194

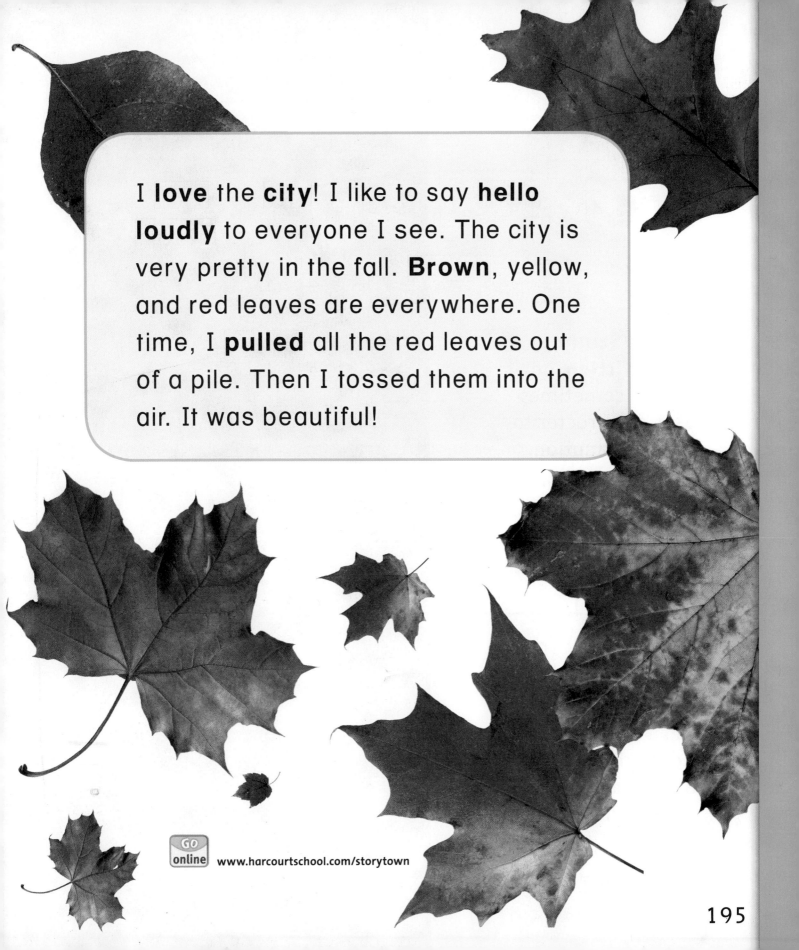

I **love** the **city**! I like to say **hello loudly** to everyone I see. The city is very pretty in the fall. **Brown**, yellow, and red leaves are everywhere. One time, I **pulled** all the red leaves out of a pile. Then I tossed them into the air. It was beautiful!

GO online www.harcourtschool.com/storytown

On Saturday
by Nina Crews

Nonfiction

Genre Study
In nonfiction, an author sometimes uses a character to give information.

Who I Met	What I Did

Comprehension Strategy

Answer Questions

Answering questions helps you understand a story better.

On Saturday

by
Nina
Crews

On Saturday, the sun shone down on the tree branches outside my window. Birds chirped loudly. They woke me up.

My mother came in. "It's a beautiful day, Jack. Get up. I'll make you toast."

On Saturday, the sun shone down on the sidewalk. Mr. Jones swept fall leaves into a big pile. The leaves were red, yellow, green, and brown. The wind blew the leaves as he swept. They whirled around and around.

"This wind keeps making more work for me," said Mr. Jones.

My mother and I helped him. People like to help each other on our block.

On Saturday, the sun shone down on Kofi's steps. He sang of people and of places. He sang of hopes and dreams.

"In Africa, people love music," he said. "They play music all the time."

We love music and we love his songs. We sang along.

On **Saturday**, the sun shone down
on Jean's dog, Rose. "Let's all take a walk,"
I said. I rubbed Rose's nose.

"You are good with dogs," said Jean.

"One day, I hope to have a dog, too," I said.

204

On Saturday, the sun shone down on
Jeff's bike.

"Hello, Jack. It's a good day for a long ride,"
he said. Jeff looked at his wheels. Leaves
were stuck between the spokes.
He pulled them out. Then off he rode.

On Saturday, the sun shone down on the food at the farmer's market. It shone down on the fruit and vegetables. The farmer had a lot to sell. He drives here on Saturdays in his big truck.

We chose apples and beans.
"Thank you," said the farmer.
"See you next Saturday!"

On Saturday, the sun shone down on the birds, the city sidewalks, the trees, the cars, and the people walking by.

We went to the park.
I kicked my soccer ball.
This is where I live.
This is the place I call home.

Think Critically

1. Is Jack happy living in his neighborhood? How do you know? DRAW CONCLUSIONS

2. Name some ways people are kind to each other. DETAILS

3. How can you tell that Jack lives in a city neighborhood? MAKE INFERENCES

4. How can you tell that Kofi is proud of Africa? DRAW CONCLUSIONS

5. **WRITE** Write about a friendly person in your neighborhood. WRITING RESPONSE

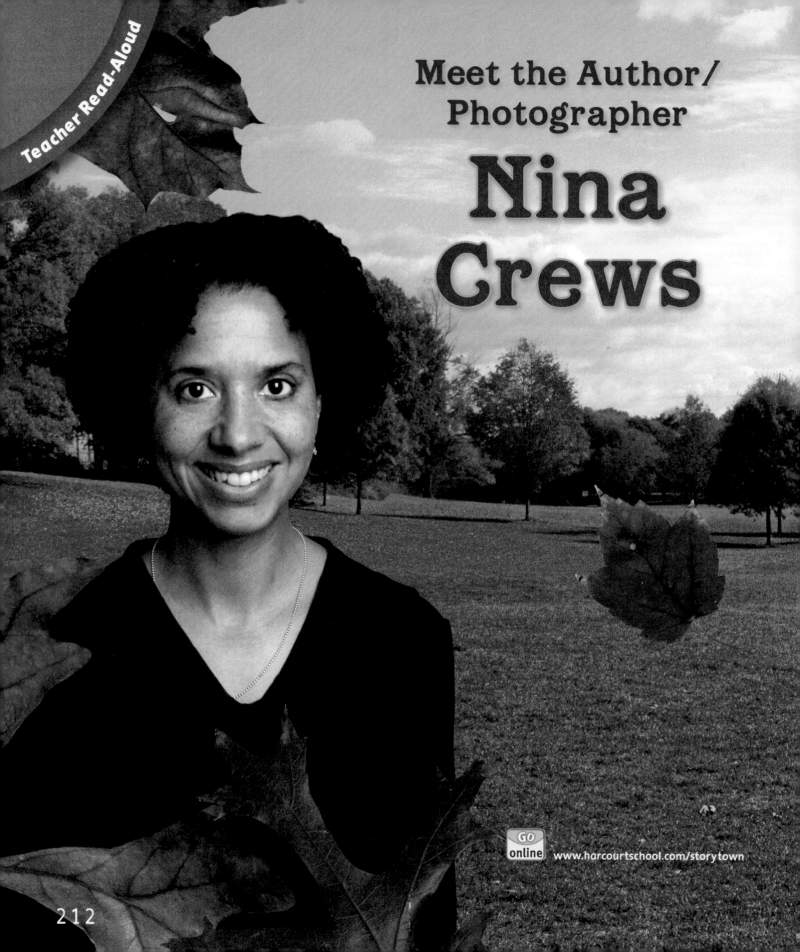

Meet the Author/
Photographer
Nina Crews

GO online www.harcourtschool.com/storytown

212

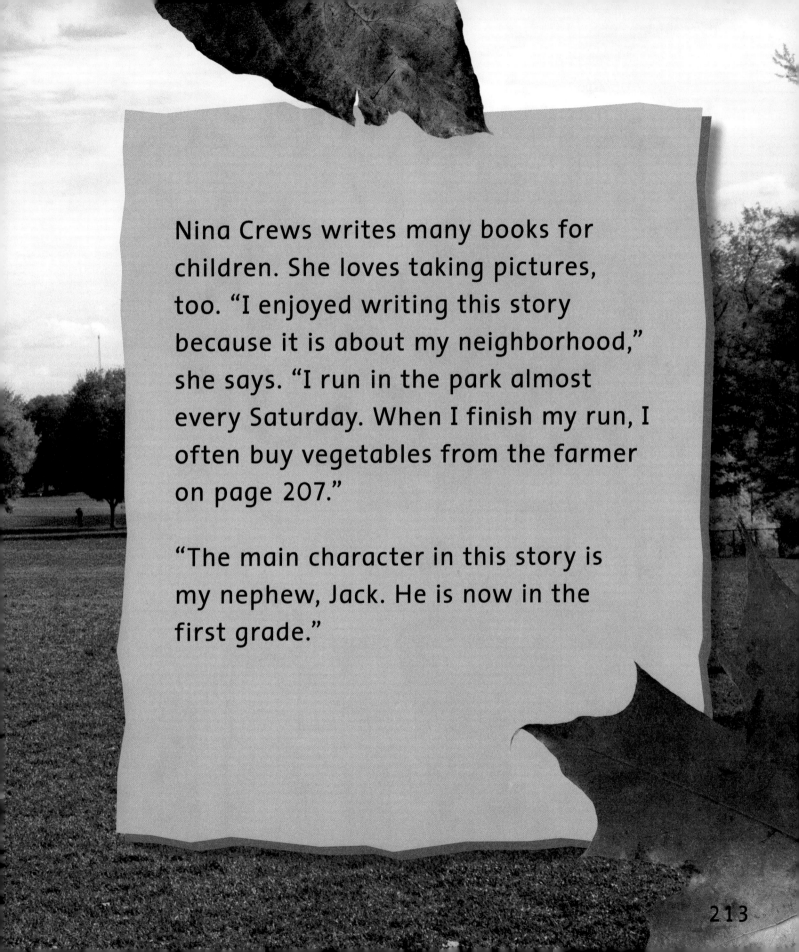

Nina Crews writes many books for children. She loves taking pictures, too. "I enjoyed writing this story because it is about my neighborhood," she says. "I run in the park almost every Saturday. When I finish my run, I often buy vegetables from the farmer on page 207."

"The main character in this story is my nephew, Jack. He is now in the first grade."

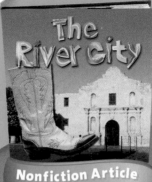

The River City

San Antonio is called the River City because the San Antonio River runs through it. The Alamo is in San Antonio. The Alamo is an important place to the people of Texas. Can you find San Antonio on the map?

TEXAS

San Antonio

MEXICO

People who come to visit San Antonio like to visit the River Walk. They can take a boat ride on the river and shop and eat at places along its bank.

The San Antonio Zoo has many kinds of animals. It was one of the first zoos to show animals not living in cages. It has one of the largest groups of birds anywhere in the world!

People come from other places to live and work in San Antonio. That's because San Antonio is a large city with jobs and homes for many people.

Connections

Comparing Texts

1 How are the neighborhoods in the story and the article the same?

2 Tell about some people and places in your neighborhood.

3 What do you like to do in your neighborhood on Saturdays?

Writing

Think about the people Jack visits. Then think of someone you like to visit. Write to tell what that person is like.

My grandpa is nice. He likes to read to me. He is very funny. Grandpa always tells me jokes.

216

Make and read new words.

Start with **bone**.

Change **b** to **c**.

Change **n** to **d**.

Change **c** to **r**.

Change **d** to **s**.

Fluency Practice

Read the story aloud with a partner. When you see a comma, stop for just a second. Stop longer for a period. When you see a question mark, read as if you are asking a question.

Contents

Lesson 24

1 Get Started **Story**

What Is in the Hedge?

by Sandra Widener
illustrated by Chris Lensch

2 Genre: Realistic Fiction

Mystery of the Night Song

by Eloise Greenfield

illustrated by
Frank Morrison

Make Some Music

3 Genre: Nonfiction Article

Phonics

Words with <u>g</u> and <u>dge</u>

Words to Know

Review

light

gone

tired

open

loudly

found

What Is in the Hedge?

by Sandra Widener
illustrated by Chris Lensch

Six yellow birds lived inside a hedge
in a backyard. They sat beside each
other on a long ledge.

The day ended, and the light was gone.
The tired birds were snug in the nest.
They each wore a cap and went to sleep.

Then came a loud Crunch! Snap! Crack!
Each bird was now awake! Each beak was
open wide.

Crack! Crunch! Snap!

What is in the hedge? What is keeping six yellow birds wide awake? What is cracking and snapping so loudly?

Marge was the bravest bird. She leaped
off the nest and rushed into the hedge.
She found that cracking, crunching snap.

225

Five birds waited for brave Marge.
"Is it a fox? Is it a cat? Is it a large hedgehog?
What is it? Tell us!" chirped the birds.

Marge rested on the ledge. "It's just rabbits!" she sang. "Those rabbits are good, so we can curl up in our nest and go back to sleep."

Focus Skill

 Draw Conclusions

Sometimes readers must use clues to figure things out in stories. Figuring things out this way is called **drawing conclusions.**

In this picture we can draw the conclusion that these people are running a race.

Clues:

· People are running on a track.

· They are wearing numbers.

Look at the picture.

What is your conclusion? What clues helped you?

Look at the picture. What is your conclusion? What clues helped you?

 www.harcourtschool.com/storytown

229

Words to Know

remembered

visitor

high

become

busy

listen

talk

eyes

Hooray! I just **remembered** something. A **visitor** is coming to see me. She is flying here with her mom. They are **high** up in the sky now. The plane will land soon. My visitor's name is Jen. We have **become** such good friends. We will be so **busy** playing when she gets here. I love to **listen** to her **talk**. Her **eyes** sparkle when she smiles. Jen is very nice!

GO online www.harcourtschool.com/storytown

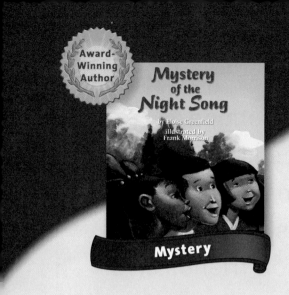

Mystery

Genre Study

Mystery stories often begin with something unusual happening. Then characters follow clues to solve the mystery.

Clues	What I Think

Comprehension Strategy

Monitor Comprehension: Make Inferences As you read, think about the clues the author has left for you.

Mystery of the Night Song

by Eloise Greenfield

illustrated by
Frank Morrison

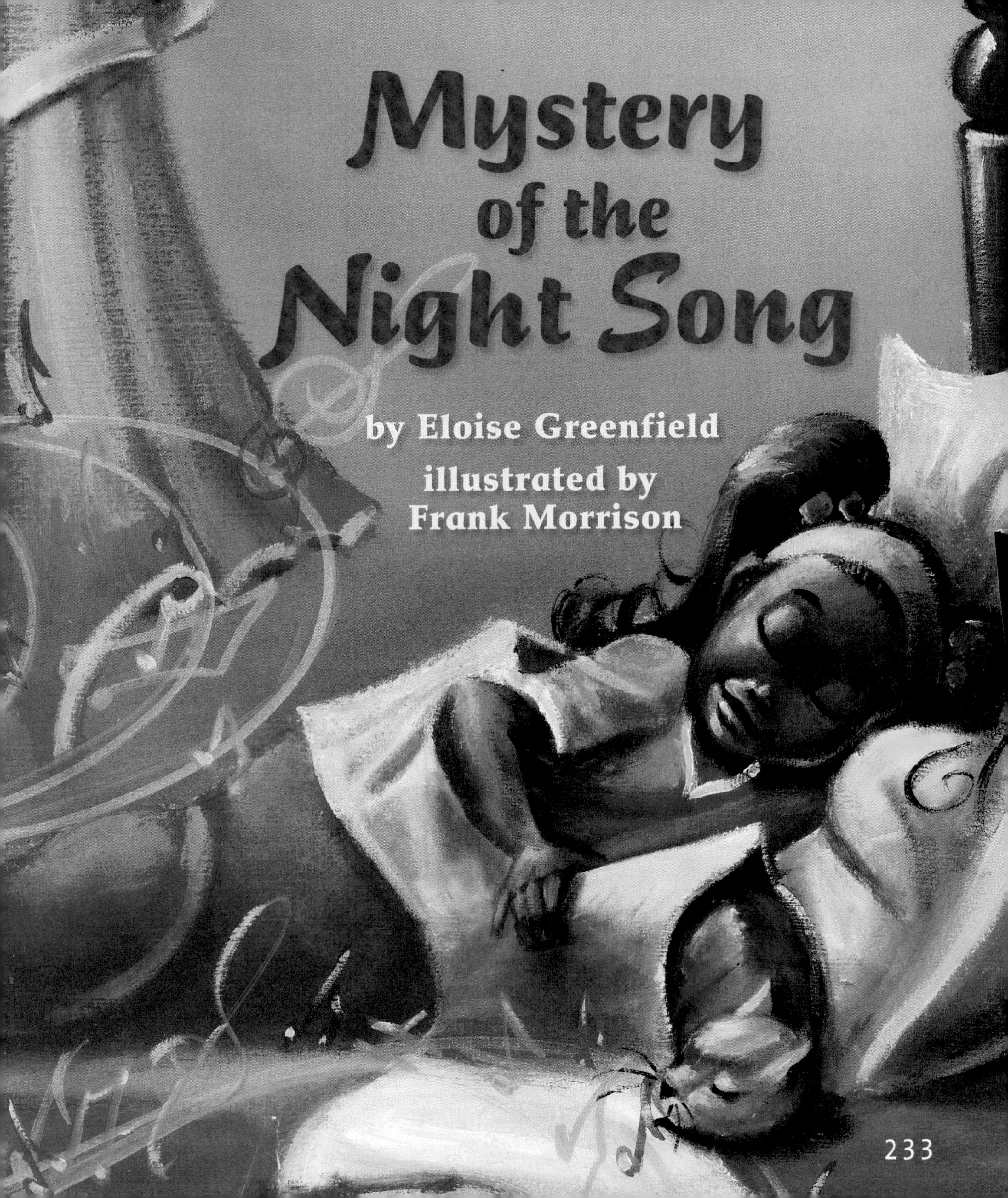

Ann was in bed.

She closed her **eyes**. The window was open.
Ann felt the fresh air.

Someone was singing.

"Night sky, night sky," she sang.

The beautiful song floated inside. When the song ended, Ann fell asleep.

The next day Ann played in Kate's backyard.
Roger was there, too.

"Did you hear someone sing last night?"
Ann asked.

"I did," Kate said.

"So did I," Roger said. "Who was it?"

"I don't know," Ann said.

"It's a mystery!" Kate said.
She was excited.

237

"Maybe it was a neighbor," Ann said. "Let's talk to the neighbors. We can ask what they were doing last night."

"I'll ask Mom, too."

"Why?" Roger asked. "Wouldn't you know if it were your mom?"

"I would," Ann said. She giggled. "But I'll have fun asking her."

239

Ann rang her own doorbell. Her mom came to the door.

"Mrs. Tucker?" Ann said. "What were you doing last night?"

Her mom smiled. "I was busy making badges for my class," she said.

"Aha!" Kate said.

"Aha, what?" Roger asked. "Do you have a clue?"

"No," Kate said. "I just like to say that!"

The children went to
three other places.

"I was playing ball with
my cat," Mrs. Sturge said.

242

"I came home very late,"
Mrs. Price said. "Then I
went to bed."

"I was cleaning my bird's cage," Mrs. Lane said.

"Aha!" Kate said.

"What is it?" asked Mrs. Lane.

"Oh, forget it," said Roger. "She just likes to say that."

243

The children went back to Kate's yard.

"Maybe it was someone walking by," Roger said.

"No," Ann said. "The song would have become softer and softer."

Roger jumped up. "Let's listen to everyone sing," he said.

The children went to each place again.
No one sang like the night singer.
One sang too high. One sang too low.
One hummed. One screeched.
One sang like a bird.

The children went back to Kate's yard again.
They sat down. Then Ann remembered something.

"I saw a large black bag in Mrs. Price's house,"
Ann said. "Maybe someone is visiting her. Let's go
and check."

The children went to Mrs. Price's house.

"Is someone visiting you?" Kate asked.

"My sister is visiting," Mrs. Price said.

"Did she sing last night?" Roger asked.

"I don't know," Mrs. Price said. "I came home very late." She called her sister to the door.

"Did you sing last night?" Ann asked.

249

"I did, indeed," the visitor said.
"The sky was so beautiful."

Ann and Roger looked at Kate. She looked
back at them. Then she giggled. "Aha!"
she said. "Aha!"

Then the singer sang her song.
The children closed their eyes and smiled.

Think Critically

1. How can you tell that Kate likes to be silly? DRAW CONCLUSIONS

2. How can you tell that these children are good thinkers? MAKE INFERENCES

3. What clue helped them solve the mystery? MAKE INFERENCES

4. What makes you think that the neighbors enjoy helping the children? DRAW CONCLUSIONS

5. **WRITE** Think of a mystery you have solved. Write about it. WRITING RESPONSE

251

Meet the Author
Eloise Greenfield

Eloise Greenfield enjoys writing stories that make the reader chuckle. "When I was in first grade I liked to read, play games with friends, and laugh with my mother," she says.

Eloise Greenfield says, "If you like to write, you should read a lot. Pay attention to the way words sound and what they mean. Try to find just the right words to say what you mean."

Meet the Illustrator
Frank Morrison

Frank Morrison has been drawing since he was a baby. When he was in the first grade, he loved to draw racecars and super heroes. He thought about his daughter and her friends when he was drawing the characters in "Mystery of the Night Song." Frank Morrison says, "Have fun with art!"

Make Some Music

Nonfiction Article

Make Some Music

Some people make music by singing. Others play instruments. There are many kinds of musical instruments.

You blow into a <u>brass</u> instrument. Air in the long tubes makes low sounds. Air in the short tubes makes high sounds.

You blow into a <u>woodwind</u> instrument, too. The "wind" you blow makes the air inside vibrate. This makes a sound.

You pluck, strum, or bow a <u>stringed</u> instrument. The strings vibrate. This makes a sound.

You hit or shake a <u>rhythm</u> instrument to make it vibrate. This makes a sound.

People all over the world enjoy music. What kinds of music do you like?

255

Connections

Comparing Texts

❶ How is the story about music? What does the article say about music?

❷ Have you ever heard someone who was a good singer? Tell about it.

❸ The children had fun solving the mystery. What do you like to do for fun?

Writing

Ann, Kate, and Roger solved a mystery. Write about a mystery that you would like to solve.

I want to find out what animal leaves footprints near my home at night.

Phonics

Make and read new words.

Start with **badge**.

Take away | b | and | d |.

Change | g | to | c |.

Put | f | at the beginning.

Change | f | to | r |.

Fluency Practice

Read the story with a partner. The characters in this story ask a lot of questions. When you read a question, make your voice sound as if you are asking a question.

Glossary

What Is a Glossary?

A glossary can help you read a word. You can look up the word and read it in a sentence. Some words have a picture to help you.

write Jane likes to **write** letters.

A

a•round   The dog ran **around** the tree.

B

be•cause   I'm sad **because** my arm hurts.

be•come   The game will soon **become** easy.

brown

brown   The dog is **brown.**

bus•y   My mom is always **busy** at work.

C

cit•y   The **city** is beautiful at night.

city

259

cool   In the fall, it gets **cool**.

 D
---

dear   Oh, **dear**! I am going to be late.

door

door   She is shutting the **door.**

dry   The wet cloth needs to **dry**.

E
---

eyes   The baby has big, brown **eyes.**

eyes

F
---

found   He **found** a sock under the bed.

four   There are **four** marbles.

four

––––––––––– **G** –––––––––––

gone   The boat is **gone** from the dock.

––––––––––– **H** –––––––––––

hears   Todd **hears** the birds chirp.

hel•lo   I say **hello** when someone calls.

high

high   The bird is flying **high.**

holes   You can cut **holes** in ice to fish.

light

love

mother

hur•ry   Let's **hurry** so we will not be late.

L
---

light   Turn on the **light.**

lis•ten   Please **listen** to me.

loud•ly   Can you whistle **loudly**?

love   I **love** you.

M
---

moth•er   Jay is with his **mother.**

move Carl helps Jess **move** a big clock.

 N

near The pond is **near** the park.

 O

o•pen The purse is **open.**

open

 P

place The desert is a dry **place.**

pulled I **pulled** my socks up.

R

re•mem•bered   Beth **remembered** to feed the cat.

right   All **right**. It's your turn now.

sky

S

should   You **should** go to bed now.

sky   Look at the beautiful **sky!**

talk

T

talk   Rob and Mike like to **talk.**

those   Can you see **those** birds in the sky?

tired   The firefighter is **tired.**

told   Ben's mom **told** him to brush his teeth.

tired

V
---

vis•i•tor   A **visitor** came to my house.

W
---

walked   We all **walked** to school.

walked

warm   A coat keeps me **warm** in the winter.

265

Acknowledgments

For permission to reprint copyrighted material, grateful acknowledgment is made to the following sources:

Bayard Presse Canada Inc.: Adapted from "Six Reasons Why Pets are Great" (Retitled: "Three Reasons Why Pets are Great") by Tanya Marissen in *chickaDEE* Magazine, October 2002.

John Berg: Cover illustration by John Berg from *chickaDEE* Magazine, October 2002.

The Cricket Magazine Group, a division of Carus Publishing Company: From "Beaks Eat" illustrated by Diane Blasius in *Click* Magazine, March 2006. Text copyright © 2006 by Carus Publishing Company; illustrations copyright © 2006 by Diane Blasius.

HarperCollins Publishers: We're Going on a Picnic! by Pat Hutchins. Copyright © 2002 by Pat Hutchins.

Marian Reiner, on behalf of the Boulder Public Library Foundation: "Houses" from *Up the Windy Hill* by Aileen Fisher. Text copyright © 1953 by Aileen Fisher; text © renewed 1981 by Aileen Fisher.

Photo Credits

Placement Key: (t) top; (b) bottom; (l) left; (r) right; (c) center; (bg) background; (fg) foreground; (i) inset

12 (t) Illustration Works; 24 (t) Desiree Walstra/Shutterstock; 25 (br) Masterfile Royalty Free; 50 (b) Patrick Bernard/Getty Images; 50 (br) PhotoAlto/SuperStock; 50 (t) Ross M Horowitz/Getty Images; 51 (tc) age fotostock/SuperStock; 51 (cl) Hein van den Heuvel/zefa/Corbis; 51 (tl) Mauritius/SuperStock; 51 (c) Royalty-Free/Corbis; 53 Stockdisc/SuperStock; 70 David Rosenberg/Getty Images; 72 (br) Photographers Choice/Getty Images; 72 (tr) Richard Bickel/Corbis; 73 (bl) Brooke Slezak/Getty Images; 73 (br) Caroline Penn/Corbis; 73 (cr) Gary Cralle/Getty Images; 73 (tr) Jim Erickson/Corbis; 74 (cl) David Rosenberg/Getty Images; 74 (br) Photographers Choice/Getty Images; 75 (tl) John Banagan/Getty Images; 75 (br) Kazuyoshi Nomachi/Corbis; 76 (c) Kazuyoshi Nomachi/Corbis; 77 (bl) Charlie Westerman/Getty Images; 77 (tr) Mark Richards/ZUMA/Corbis; 78 (c) Yadid Levy/Alamy; 79 (t) Jim Erickson/Corbis; 80 (c) Martin Harbvey/Corbis; 81 (b) Caroline Penn/Corbis; 81 (tr) Michele Falzone/Alamy; 82 (tl) Richard Bickel/Corbis; 82 (br) Wolfgang Kaehler/Corbis; 83 (tl) Jodi Hilton/Corbis; 83 (br) Michael Melford/The Image Bank/Getty Images; 84 (cr) Galen Rowell/Corbis; 84 (bg) Gary Cralle/Getty Images; 85 (cr) David Hiser/Stone/Getty Images; 85 (tl) Jean Pragen/Getty Images; 86 (br) Joe Cornish/Getty Images; 86 (t) Lenora Gim/Getty Images; 87 (cl) Brooke Slezak/Getty Images; 87 (cr) Bryan & Cherry Alexander Photography; 88 (tl) Gary Vestal/Getty Images; 88 (tr) Gary Vestal/Getty Images; 88 (bl) Gary Vestal/Getty Images; 88 (br) Gary Vestal/Getty Images; 89 (t) Ariel Skelley/Getty images; 89 (br) Greg Ceo/Getty Image; 90 (c) Patrick Molnar/Getty Images; 91 (t) Digital Vision/Getty Images; 92 (inset) Frank Krahmer/The Image Bank/Getty Images; 92 (b) Ryan McVay/Stone/Getty Images; 93 (tr) Bruno Levy/zefa/Corbis; 93 (bc) Frans Lemmens/zefa/Corbis; 96 age fotostock/SuperStock; 108 (bl) Royalty-Free/Corbis; (c) BananaStock/Alamy; (br) PhotoDisc/Getty Images; (t) Simone van den Berg/Shutterstock; 109 (t) Brand X/SuperStock; 134 (b) Blend Images/Alamy; 135 (cr) Christina Kennedy/Alamy; 135 (bl) Coneyl Jay/Getty Images; 136 Johanna Goodyear RF/Shutterstock; 137 age fotostock/SuperStock; 193 (br) age fotostock/SuperStock; 214 (bg) Dan Holmberg/Photonica/Getty Images; 214 (b) Kazumi Nagasawa/amana images/Getty Images; (bg) Panoramic Images/Getty Images; (b) Royalty-Free/Corbis; 215 (t) age fotostock/SuperStock; 215 (t) David Butow/Corbis; (b) Grant Faint/The Image Bank/Getty Images; (b) Jeffery Allan Salter/Corbis Saba; (t) Jerry Amster/SuperStock; (c) John Giustina/Taxi/Getty Images; (c) Robert Benson; (b) Sandy Felsenthal/Corbis; (c) Walter Bibikow/Taxi/Getty Images; 216 Shutterstock; 217 Frances Roberts/Alamy; 229 (br) Purestock/Alamy; (tl) The Garden Picture Library/Alamy; 254 (bl) Pat Doyle/Corbis; (c) Photodisc/Getty Images; 255 (tl) C Squared Studios/ Getty Images; (cl) Image Source/Getty Images; (cr) Mary Grace Long/Getty Images; (br)

Richard Kolker/Getty Images; (bl) Stockbyte/Getty Images; 256 (bg) Losevsky Pavel/Shutterstock; 257 (br) Masterfile Royalty Free.

All other photos © Harcourt School Publishers. Harcourt photos provided by Harcourt Index, Harcourt IPR, and Harcourt Photographers: Weronica Ankarorn, Eric Camden, Doug DuKane, Ken Kinsie, April Riehm and Steve Williams.

Illustration Credits

Cover Art; Laura and Eric Ovresat, Artlab, Inc.